Galaxie Wagon

DARNELL ARNOULT

Galaxie Wagon

POEMS

LOUISIANA STATE UNIVERSITY PRESS

BATON ROUGE

Published by Louisiana State University Press
Copyright © 2016 by Darnell Arnoult
All rights reserved
Manufactured in the United States of America
LSU Press Paperback Original
First printing

DESIGNER: *Mandy McDonald Scallan*
TYPEFACE: *Whitman*

Grateful acknowledgment is made to the editors of the following publications, in which the poems listed first appeared, sometimes in slightly different form and sometimes with a different title: *2013 Anthology of Appalachian Writers, Gretchen Moran Laskas Volume V:* "Gravity"; *Appalachian Heritage:* "Body," "Deed," "Lining Out," "Of Love," "Promise," and "Singularity"; *Motif V3: Work:* "December"; *Now and Then Magazine:* "Trail"; *Seminary Ridge Review:* "Church"; *Southern Cultures:* "The Gorilla Story"; *The Southern Poetry Anthology, Volume VI: Tennessee:* "Hiding," "Lining Out," and "While You Are Away"; *The Southern Poetry Anthology, Volume VII: North Carolina:* "Change" and "Galaxie Wagon." "Promise" is for Virginia Elizabeth Stone. "The Letter V" is for Vivian Blake Stone. "Bedtime" is for Emerson Mae Stone. "Apart" is for William.

"Into the Stone" (excerpt) from *The Whole Motion: Collected Poems, 1945–1992,* by James Dickey © 1992. Reprinted with permission of Wesleyan University Press.

Library of Congress Cataloging-in-Publication Data
Arnoult, Darnell, 1955–
 [Poems. Selections]
 Galaxie wagon : poems / Darnell Arnoult.
   pages ; cm
 ISBN 978-0-8071-6281-1 (pbk. : alk. paper) — ISBN 978-0-8071-6282-8 (pdf) — ISBN 978-0-8071-6383-2 (epub) — ISBN 978-0-8071-6284-2 (mobi)
 I. Title.
 PS3601.R586A6 2016
 811'.6—dc23

2015033303

The paper in this book meets the guidelines for permanence and durability of the Committee on Production Guidelines for Book Longevity of the Council on Library Resources.♾

FOR COWBOY

Through the stone held in air by my heartbeat.
My thin flesh is shed by my shadow;
My hair has turned white with a thought.

—JAMES DICKEY, from "Into the Stone"

CONTENTS

Acknowledgments XI

Singularity 1

The Gorilla Story 2

Imaginary Art 4

Southside Pool, June 1959 6

Writing Lessons 7

Hospitality 8

Planting Phlox 9

Change 10

Her Real Name Was Peaches 11

Expatriate 12

Seamstress 13

Promise 14

MG 15

Of Love 18

Gravity 19

Old Feet 21

Baggage 22

Episodes 23

Wild Card 25

Love Story 26

Call and Response 28

Ars Poetica—
Baxter, Tenn. 30

Predawn 31

How I Came to Saddle a Horse
at the Bar J 32

Ode to the Dixie Pig—
Business 220 34

Note 35

Lining Out 36

Deed 37

Honeymoon near Oneida 38

Little Farm 39

Hiding 40

Trail 42

Two in the Morning 43

Body 44

Apart 45

Blood 46

Fear 47

CONTENTS

Terrain 48

Napping 49

December 50

Fire 52

The Letter V 54

Forest of Wordless Words 55

Spoons 56

Portent 57

Mean Time 58

After the Hurricane 59

Altar 61

Harmonic Mean 62

Church 64

Bedtime 65

Mystery Rules 66

Galaxie Wagon 67

ACKNOWLEDGMENTS

I am grateful to Lincoln Memorial University for the time, support, and accommodation generously extended for the writing of this book and to my colleagues, friends, and students there who have played a part in that generosity. Thanks also to the Hobson Foundation and Chowan University.

I would also like to thank John Easterly, MaryKatherine Callaway, Catherine Kadair, Mandy McDonald Scallan, Erin Rolfs, Jennifer Keegan, and others at LSU Press who helped make this book possible. Thank you, Denton Loving, Patti Meredith, Tom Rankin, Lee Smith, Iris Tillman Hill, Lucinda MacKethan, Connie Green, Sue Dunlap, Tony Maxwell and Joe Wolfenbarger, Aaron Smith, Belinda Smith, Ben and Janice Lynch, Bruce and Vivian Sevier, Joseph Bathanti, Jesse Graves, Maurice Manning, George Ella Lyon, Judy Goldman, Abigail DeWitt, Sue Richardson Orr, Joyce MacDonald, Vicki Brumback, Carol Grametbauer, Kathryn Stripling Byer, Geneil Dillehay, Jim Minick, Robert Gipe, Georgann Eubanks and Donna Campbell, Luther Kirk, George Singleton, Michael Chitwood, Sylvia Lynch, Cary Holladay, John Bensko, Kristin Inversen, Rebecca Skloot, Richard Bausch, Tom Russell, Dana Wildsmith, Jane Hicks, Sara West, Wendy Dinwiddie, Hannah Henry, Marcus Burchfield, Chasiddy Wright, JP Russell, Pamela Duncan, Kory Wells, Phyllis Grayson, Rebecca Flippen, and Sudie LeGrey. Most of all, I thank my family for their continued support and love, particularly Beth and Alex, Chad and Jody, Virginia, Vivian, Emerson, and Xander. Also Darryl and Amy Brock and their families, particularly Lauren Brock. With special gratitude to Dottie Arnoult. Endless thanks to my beloved husband and cowboy, the man in the cards, William Brock.

Galaxie Wagon

Singularity

Heaven is in the dark.
Reposes in the silent dark.

The slim emptiness sliding
between. Slip-sliding

between all things—Heaven.
In the buoyancy of Heaven

a bell strikes. It tings.
Pools. And the light tings

and pools in the seed
and seam. The seed,

the light seed has a voice.
Do we begin with a voice?

The Gorilla Story

Around ten, the phone rang. We were all in bed. I was two.
"Joe," he heard the voice slur. "There's a fellow with a gorilla

down here. Says he'll pay a hundred bucks to anybody
who goes five minutes with his monkey and walks out

under his own steam." Daddy said, "Where is he?"
into the black receiver, heavy enough itself to be a weapon.

Between bed and the bazaar, he drank a fifth of liquor
and still had to pay fifty cents more to be foolish.

Daddy wore a coat and tie when he wasn't playing golf—
even to fight gorillas. The gorilla caught him

by the necktie. Dragged him through peanut hulls,
banana peels, slides of excrement, then tossed Daddy

to the back of the cage and rattled the bars
to scare onlookers and earn his pay. But Daddy

came to and leaped onto the gorilla's back and grabbed
the bars just beyond all that hair and muscle. Pinned him

to his own cage. Daddy held on until he walked out under his own steam.
He held out his hand for the hundred, but the carney wasn't having it.

"You had an illegal hold on my gorilla!" the man barked.
"How," my daddy said from that night until the day he died,

"can a man have an illegal hold on something with four hands?"
Forty years later, I met a boxing chimpanzee named Congo,

a champion in '57. He'd retired to Tarpon Springs. Someone wrote a book
about him, *The Gorilla Show*. I have this poem. He outlived Daddy

by at least twenty years. Congo never talked about that night in Martinsville, ashamed to have been beaten. Not even to me. My daddy on the other hand

won years of telling this story. He taught me to tell it, that it's a story worth believing, even with no proof but the story itself.

Imaginary Art

—AFTER LISEL MUELLER

1. How I Would Sculpt Imagination

It would be a child's body, clothed,
seen from the sides and rear. She would
peer into the granite block
she is made from, her face still
part of the monolith she looks into
to see all the women she might become,
all the directions she might take
when she backs away and steps
down from the white pedestal
and walks past the red velvet ropes.

2. How I Would Sculpt Art

Gray walls with a hint of olive
or eggplant, a dark plain palm
holding vivid rectangles of bright
marbles glistening with days
and weeks, all the Crayola swirls
of living in an instant, a raindrop
of blood, a snowflake of breath,
a bleat, a blink, a snap, a snatch, a snare.

3. How I Would Sculpt Beauty

A figure of a woman at a small sink
in the only bathroom of a house
on Chestnut Street. She would stare,
open-mouthed, into the medicine
chest mirror, rubbing her spit
with the small black brush
into the tar of Maybelline mascara,
one set of eyelashes already done,
her lips already scarlet, the mole

near the crease of her smile
already brushed black, marking
her loveliness. It would be
my mother in marble,
before her real troubles,
frozen in her mid-thirties, when she
looked like a star.

4. How I Would Sculpt Idea

Pieces of crinkled copper pages
in different stages of wadding
beside a stainless steel trashcan
overflowing with wadded, crinkled
copper paper, one open on the stone
pedestal floor, having missed its target,
cupping its contents like the hand
of someone asleep, the fingers
of the page still curved up and loosely
holding, still hiding $E = mc^2$, or perhaps
a draft of this poem.

5. How I Would Sculpt Supper

A pine table covered by a white cotton tablecloth,
dotted with petals from spring perennials,
the vase sea green, the petals sapphire.
Old white china veined in fine gray cracks,
polished silver-plated flatware, something
ornate, cut milk-glass goblets, one chipped.
The plates full of perfect blocks of meatloaf,
pebbles of spring peas, and a cloud
of whipped potatoes—all of it lovely
and too delicious to eat.

Southside Pool, June 1959

I glide through the water at Southside pool,
across the black bars that shine between rows

and rows of pale concrete, my four-year-old
body launched into blue-green fluid

of three-feet, into liquid air. So smooth,
so cool. My hands crossed, palms down, point beyond

my head, piercing the blur before me. Eyes
sting but stay open. Elbows find my ears.

Everything I believe I am points to
you, the man stepping backward. I watch you

ease away at the same time your ready
hands extend to me below the surface.

They curl and extend, coax me farther than
before, signal arms and legs to churn, churn

in rhythm, slice the water with the heart
you have given me. Only mid-waking

I gasp for breath. In that threshold tick of
the dreamer's clock, my arrowed hands graze tips

of your fingers, their eternal promise.
And so I churn, hold my breath beneath the

surface, working and waiting, immersed in
this watery world, until I reach you.

Writing Lessons

He holds the pen
in his practiced hand.

Letters stream even and
orderly from my father's

wand of words across
lineless pages, where

they lie—sweet and
graceful—in form and

function. The last letter
of his name a rakish

flourish. Like mine.
Letters in his hand—

fountain-blue steps
on white rag snow.

Hospitality

When Fear comes knocking like a Fuller Brush man,
you let him in and pour him coffee, you know him
so well. You give him real cream. Offer pound cake.

He usually declines. He opens his valise and draws out
all he has to show you, even though you already know
his line. How can you live without his brushes?

They keep your life clean and groomed. Sometimes you
consider hiding behind the drapes and letting him peek
in the side lights at the front door. Let him think

he's missed you, that you left too soon. But then,
he might have just what you don't know you need,
a new letter opener, some new kind of vegetable brush,

a whisk broom that fits in your purse, goes where you go.
You grab a dishtowel, rush to the door, turn the knob.
You make up some lie you were washing dishes

or making potato leek soup. You say, you almost missed
his knock. But you don't miss anything. He's regular.
Regular as the calendar that ticks the days away.

So you get the coffee and the cream. You take sugar
in yours to cut the bitter taste, and then you always
gaze into the open box and buy something he's selling.

Planting Phlox

Creeping
Phlox, the carpet
of Heaven. Smell summer
coming. Subulata—Latin
for awl,
for it's
needle-shaped leaves.
Phlox—Greek for flame. Craves sun.
Often mistaken for thrift. Smell
the spring.
Mother
worked on her knees,
troweling, tossing rust red
clay from small empty wounds near curb's
edge. Smell
summer
coming. Each clutch
a spiny-leaved beauty,
sets already blossoming pink
and white
five-point
stars. Phlox fragrant
with bright April. Its ghost,
Pentecost. Also mistaken
for thrift.
Without
hose or pail, or
watering can, we quenched
thirsty bouquets with sloshes from
a chipped
Ball jar.
By kiss of our
hands, we soothed the scars.
Mother, daughter, phlox, all thirsted
for more.

Change

Mother's courting parlor made a bedroom
when all the courting was done. No heat
but for a small woodstove used to burn paper.

No air-conditioning except to pry
open stuck, over-painted, double-hung
windows that shook in glossy white sashes

like old bones. Nobody opened the door
to the outside anymore. Somebody
put a table in front of it. Sheer white

priscillas slung crosshatched over lead glass,
sagging bridal veils. In summer we slept in
twin beds, only starched cotton sheets to wick

away sweat. Come winter, we carted the twins
out to the storage shed and carried back
a poor-man's iron bed, tubular steel, flat

springs. We slept front to back in the valley
under a stack of quilts heavy to heave
off as the house. Dreams and visions hovered

round our bed like white-hot stars,
hers hallucinations and delusions,
mine a death grip on a future away

from where I slept. Like a rock step, we rolled
over in unison when a back grew cold.
Now I dream of that room and the chill

of the floor in winter, the cloud of my breath,
how our lives took shape from need out of reach,
beyond the yoke of something as simple as yearning.

Her Real Name Was Peaches

Madame Natasha's ringed hands show
their age, like mine. The cards are worn,

faded red to pink and slick. Her deck and hands
make hushed sounds as she shuffles

and slides each day, here, there, and yet,
to the tabletop. A hidden face, my life

spreads across beautiful paper slabs,
stones on a path. In the center—what is,

below—what was and what pushes and pulls,
above—what comes and what comes again,

if I don't change my ways. *Here,* she says,
is the Tower. You will be reborn. Here,

she says, *is cups, that is love.* I consider
love in all its renderings. The lotus, the water,

the two goblets. I reach and pluck a card
from her deck. I say, *Try this one.* I take

another. *And this one,* I say. I lay my choices
over each she has carefully placed in my path.

Expatriate

My grandmother's place
spreads out like a country.
In the capital to the north,
her kitchen. She ruled with
the threat of fly flapper
and warm castor oil.

To the south, the apple
trees sprawl. Fruit falls
like poison pearls. Early,
inside the tart green
ornament, a puzzle piece
of bellyache still hides,

too eager to torture the
innocent. In the henhouse
beyond the swept and mowed,
near her garden-gone-
feral, chickens have been
laid off, equipment sold.

Even now, I pledge my
allegiance to the line
full of laundry whipping
in the East and search
for chinquapins and walnuts
in the wild woods west.

Seamstress

Get the dogs and horses fed.
Get the goats and chickens fed.

Mop floors and make the beds.
Sweep porch, weed iris beds.

Get collars and pockets pressed,
ready to sew. Fresh biscuits pressed

into flakey pucks. Fry eggs. Mend
socks. Tighten loose buttons. Mend

fences of broken zippers. Stitch
the day together with a whip. Stitch

together what bears holding safe
in the backstitch of daylight. Safe

basted through the seasons. Fancy
finishes so the inside is as fancy

as outside. Flat-felled seams
hide more than the seams

between, hide the mowed lines,
the scars, polish the surfaces. Lines

of clothes hammer on spring wind,
wait for sprinkle and steam. In the wind

of time, working lives shine and sleep.
Chores get done before chickens sleep.

Chain-of-snore stitches run like dogs' dreams
of squirrels. Feed dogs hound my dreams.

Promise

Spilled from the cup of your mother,
that warm body, you are the universe
in a single squirming drop. You can
still call every star by name, count

the colors in God's eyes. Bloodsongs
sing wild. Your first single syllable
slides over your sweet searching tongue.

Slender fingers work to hold, reach
and reach for the names you're already
forgetting. How many voices have you

had? To choose only one before you speak.
Two tiny stars, your eyes, already
bearing witness. I wish I could tell you
how to live, but you won't want to be told.

MG

My first car is a royal blue MG.
On a July day in the gravel drive
just a short grassy slope above a steep
red-clay hill that refuses to harbor grass

seed long enough to sprout blades,
I breathe in hot black leather,
oiled wood panels and knobs,
dusty nap of wool carpet. Chrome

glints the sun's apex, flickering
a quiet SOS as I swing the steering
wheel to and fro. I'm six years old.
My brother traded me half a Midget

for half the portable Zenith hi-fi
Santa left me. The baking tonneau
unsnapped on the driver's side, I sit toasty
and hopeful, driving toward some

unarticulated destiny imagining Elvis
at my side. In reality, I drive there alone
and often, as in this moment. Never mash
the clutch or disengage the gears. Maybe

he told me not to touch. Only to steer
in the stillness. Maybe I am blessed.
Was my brother inside, in his attic room
playing "Only the Lonely" and thinking

of the girl he'd marry? How he'd leave?
Or was he already in the Navy? Already
a gunner's mate on the USS *Newport News,*
the Gray Ghost from the East Coast,

floating on swell and trough of Jello-blue
Mediterranean? Or was he in the Gulf
of Tonkin? Time meanders. Who's
watching me? No one in my memory

knows where I am, hidden in that sweet
hollow of my brother's sapphire
sports car. A decade cruises by.
My brother sits beside me

in a colorless Ford Falcon, square-
backed and boring, no sexy torpedo
fenders. The car is so beige
it might as well be invisible except

for its five wheels and the shift. "To you,
then down," he says. "Find the sweet spot
where the clutch catches." He helped
Mother buy this already old, but not old

enough, car for me. "Worry about where
you're going, not where you are."
He points to the wild asphalt unrolling
ahead of us. "You go where you look,"

he says. July heat blows heavy as brick
in the open windows. Bland tan upholstery
weaves and pinches and embosses
the backs of my sweaty thighs. My ponytail

cuts at my eyes and mouth. My skirt
balloons up from my nervous knees.
He turns on the radio and twists
the dial to find Roy Orbison buried

deep inside some Beatles song.
The Falcon's steering wheel rocks
so large, so loose. The blocky bird
lurches up the street like a drunkard's hiccup.

He coaches me through each gear,
three on the tree, the magic H. He talks
me through each stop sign, each hill
and stall. I learn the emergency brake

trick. We buck through city limits
and swing out onto switchback two-lanes,
most without line or shoulder, until I glide
from gear to gear, slicing into the country,

windshield full of azure sky and raw cotton,
home a tiny sacred speck and shrinking.
It's disappeared. All that lethal pleasure
clutched in my lean girlish hands.

Of Love

My parents married to hear each other's stories.
Somewhere in the tunnel they stopped telling them.

Gravity

My golden retriever and I orbited the old neighborhood,
        nightly assaying the phases of the moon
cycling through glow to shadow. I felt its pull, some wave
        in me crashing. I watched for the fat harvest moon.

Louie and I entertained the idea that the man who'd come love me
        loved dogs and contemplated the same
cream ball at night, his story full as ours. His love bountiful.
        I seeded romance in signs etched by stars and moon.

My grandmother spoke of signs and wonders, planted
        in the new and the old, the waxing and the waning.
Planted what yielded above ground in the increase; root crops
        prospered in the spooning dark of the moon.

Is love a root or a flower? I have often wondered. Is it a rock
        or a stream? I've been confused. I've come clear.
Clear as the night we met halfway, in the middle of the Radisson
        lobby, anointed by that mountain man moon.

By Sunday we prepared to part ways, a snowy baptism speckling
        your hat and coat, your eyelashes. We said
we'd give it a go, try again in a month's time, a month of letters
        and longing, of waxing and waning moon.

Next time, you sat with your boots on the desk, your wire rims low
        on your nose, ponytail trailing down
your back like water, Goldsmith in your hands. Is love a wonder
        or a bargain? What is alchemy but the moon?

You, gift of heaven, riddle me days, your astrology of words
        and numbers, to solve for a fool's day for a fool's
errand—love. The groom's fire burns and casts kisses of light
        on his round-faced bride, moody woman, moon.

Above the distance that cradles, a tide of stars glistens like diamonds,
　　　like you laughing. You walk the dog
now in a neighborhood of cows and corn. Like light, yearning reflects,
　　　curls and unfurls, a perpetual honeyed moon.

Old Feet

It happened when I wasn't looking.
Brittle toenails hiding under bright pink

polish from homemade pedicures.
Insteps aching after an hour of standing

on concrete. The pumice brick hangs humbled
from the tub spigot, acknowledging its limits.

Peeling pages of so many calendars,
years of tender June days walking the gravel

driveway to the mailbox to see if I had a love
letter, sweet-talking on into August,

when the soles of my feet had come familiar
to barefoot days. My little toenails, always runts,

the tucked-in trouble makers, are pure-T lost causes.
I've stopped mollycoddling, teasing them out

long enough so I can slap them pink or scarlet
or mauve. I just paint a nail on each tiny toe and go.

Maturity embraces accommodation, consolation.
My ankle bones disappear at the end of a long day

or a good barbecue sandwich. I wonder how long
before someone else trims my toenails. Rough shod

as I am, I can't trade these dogs in.
They've stuck by me. Hell, they've stuck to me.

Baggage

The top is down.
My daughter drives
toward Virginia.
My mother,
eighty-one
next week, who
couldn't get out
of the back seat
with a crane,
rides shotgun.
I sit in back
like a suitcase
that won't fit
in the trunk—
mute and deaf
in the whipping wind.

Episodes

I longed for a cattle drive, a wagon train, a galloping palomino
with flowing mane. I wore a cowgirl outfit. Loved singing cowboys,
Roy and Gene, their trick stallions, happy-trail songs, sidekicks,
righting wrongs, saving damsels in lariated firearmed fairytales.

Then my tenderfoot attention turned to wounded cowboy noir,
snatches of story caught in perpetual rerun. Acolyte, I hunkered
at the edge of a wagon-wheel rocker, face inches from the walnut
altar, that boxy black-and-white television with its gold-speckled

fabric-covered speaker. I attended each regular saga faithfully
after geography and algebra homework. Clinched the hair trigger
of a worn-out vertical hold button steady between thumb and finger
and prayed for good reception. Handsome, war-scarred, gun-slinging,

tortured-soul counterparts, antiheros to those earlier song-sainted cowpokes,
rode the range with broken hearts—Paladin, Gil Favor, Rowdy Yates,
Bronco Layne—rakish boys gone to men, making their way, still
burdened by pall of war. Its turbulence pushed them like a cortege,

a brewing storm always on the horizon. Hardship meant nothing,
saddle and lasso their sacrament of penance. Always they tried
to sidestep the snare of temptation, despite spinning six-guns
and brutal right crosses. They pined for some gone home, their return

to family and sweethearts barred by a battle-scarred limbo, better wed
to tragedy and rootlessness. Drovers and drifters, marshals, deputies,
bounty hunters. Take scribbling Johnny Yuma, a journal, sawed-off shotgun,
or Josh Randall, that mare's leg parade, defending the wrongly accused.

Lead or drag, trail boss or ramrod, lawman or outlaw, beans or hardtack,
each day, despite their lively theme music, they lived their contrition, appeasing
ghosts and bedroll nightmares, finding their way in the dirt and dust of work
and wandering the canyoned wilderness, remuda horses turning 180s and 360s

under booms swinging high off camera. Cheyenne Bodie learned to ride
as the camera rolled. "You'll learn or die trying," they told him. Sugarfoot
searched for justice in a volume of law tucked in his saddlebag, thinking
education would change something. Death still inevitable. All doomed

to be single or quickly married and just as quickly widowed. Calamity
and salvation eked out in thirty- and sixty-minute measures. All the hours
I attended that church, real war and bloodshed lurked in the crimson canons
only a channel click away. How much you miss in syndication. I learned

to ride a brindled Appaloosa not long before I became a grandmother.
Out of season, Patch walks easy, slow, thoughtful of my old bones
on steep and rocky logging roads. My partner, he's been around
the block, knows a thing or two. I still know nothing, miss so much.

Our trails are cut by park rangers, deer hunters, four-wheeling fellows.
Far from a highway or phone line or television, I am back in time when
Pony Express packed love letters and contracts and claims in saddlebags.
I feature myself in a life I witnessed on a range of black to white.

But in these green to brown woods, yet alive and singing, bloodroot drips
against moss and loam. My husband, easy in the saddle, teaches me
about his barefoot childhood, his Muskogee granny, medicine woman,
what she knew and passed on, mysteries of her own great-great-grandmother,

a fugitive from the Trail of Tears, first rounded up in a horseshoe, Sequatchie Valley,
where my man was born. How this haunts him more than anything his Pentecostal
preacher father warned against. He points to dogbane, poke sallet, the color
of healing poisons. What sweet tension on the verge of this new season.

Wild Card

I move to leave the seer's house.
He calls me back. Clumsy,
I've knocked a card loose
from the little chair he spread
them on. *What about your love life?*
All women want to know
about their love life.
Those words don't have a road

to drive. The question no gas
in its tank. *No dog in that fight,*
I say. *I see him coming,* he tells me.
He's riding toward you, he says,
on the back of a good horse.
And I thought I was bad to use clichés.

Love Story

I first knew God in my child hands folded like a steeple,
my father's voice a kind song lining out the *Our Father*
and *Hail Mary*, the *Act of Contrition*. I was three.

I held God in my hands like a bird and when my
hands opened, He bloomed into the *Glory Be*.
Later, I knew God in the rustle of black skirts and veils

and white wimples. The click and clatter of giant rosaries,
tethered crucifixes whipping through the air with the nuns'
sure stride, the weight of their steps in those black lace-up

shoes skimming worn wooden floors, their polished faces,
traces of white chalk on their fingers and on their sleeves,
the mystery of their holiness, their orders. I knew God

in the bright vestments, gold chalice, brass bells, *Kyrie,*
the host held high in the mystical Latin tongue of the Mass.
I knew God in the broken piece of wafer that rested

on my tongue, never to touch teeth, but to hold, protected
from the bite of hunger or eagerness, until there was nothing
left but the holy aftertaste of redemption and sacrifice.

I knew God in the stories of young girl saints who saw
visions, the mystical romance. I longed for a vision.
Gradually, I came to understand that God hides

in the questions we learn to ask. A better guide
than a polished face, a touch better than a name.
I knew God in the eyes of my children coming to me

like surprise letters, their bodies in pages holy and sacred
in their unfolding. Their artful penmanship, the baptism
of their inky words as they learned them, the sweet

sentences, their first steps syllables of their days,
their first wonder. My voice lining out their prayers,
the *Our Father,* the *Hail Mary,* the *Glory Be,*

their hands holding God like a hummingbird's
breath fluttering against their paired palms.
I know Heaven as a humming orchestra now

in mid-movement, God both conductor and cymbalist,
pushing and coaxing, punctuating and pacing,
and I am an instrument, one of many. I hear God

in the giggle and gasp, the trill and the trial, the song
and the screech, the slap and rub, the waltz
and shag, the rush and retreat. I catch a glimpse

of Him in the unfolding of what we all hold
in the church of our body, the hymn of our breath,
the Sabbath of this world of shadow and stars.

Call and Response

I. Ad: November 30, 1998

Do you like horses,
fishing, sitting on the porch
watching it rain?

Do you like fine dining?
Concerts? I wear both
kinds of clothes.

Let's talk. (Signed) Cowboy

II. Response: December 1, 1998

I have fished with a cane pole, using a safety pin
for a hook. No fish.

Once upon a time I had a palomino Shetland pony
named Buck Shot.

That mean little shit threw the neighborhood kids
as often as we climbed

into the saddle. Once my daddy had to chase him for miles.
My mother cried

Buck Shot would give my daddy a heart attack. I cried
because my wanting

a palomino like Roy was going to kill my daddy. But
he trudged home,

sold the little shit, and kept the saddle, which I slung
onto the back of a sorrel

Naugahyde sleeper sofa and rode the range, saving my
walking doll from stampedes

and rising floodwaters, until my legs grew too long
and my mother began to list

too far back when she sat on the sleeper sofa to read
the evening paper.

I do enjoy rain, thunder, and watching lightning river
and tributary against the sky.

That's the time to be quiet. I like Van Morrison. *Mama told me
there'd be days like this.*

I like food just fine, and I like fine food. I appreciate a man
with good variety in his wardrobe.

I have loved cowboys all my life.
(Signed) TV Cowgirl

Ars Poetica—
Baxter, Tenn.

All day long poets
circle the small pond,
casting their lines. A great catfish—as big as any poet—reputed
to be older than both
art and words, lurks beneath the surface. He has bottom-fed in this deep
water for time on top of time.

He is fat. Savvy. Whiskers
waxed. He won't be an easy catch.
There's this fish woman. She drives
a dry-erase board around
water's edge on a Mule.

She has scales and
weighs each fisherman's
catch. There's this
contest with cash
prizes and ribbons,
things a fat cat
like that cares
nothing for.
His reward
is a plate of
cornmeal,
an iron skillet.

He will sizzle
in hot grease.
Turn golden.
It's all in the
bait, they say.

Other stanzas will include coleslaw,
white beans, onion, garlic hushpuppies, tartar sauce,
sweet tea with lemon, chocolate meringue pie. His picture in *Southern Living.*

Predawn

Windows
still black, air damp,
the dogs continue to
prowl the fence line. It is my hour
to read.
The house
holds still except
the flat-assed speckled cat,
her hind legs always in a squat
like she
landed
on her feet one
time too many. She craves
my time alone to demonstrate
her love.
Any
other time she
would balk at such wanton
affection. In graying light, grass
waits to
glisten.
Birds interrupt
the hush of fleeting night
and I brush aside this offer,
this brash
teasing
faithless love rub,
for words written in blood,
rich ripe words that
bleed and bleed and bleed onto my
hard heart.

How I Came to Saddle a Horse at the Bar J

I need to learn to ride,
I say into the phone. A friend
asked me on a week-long ride into the wilderness. (A test, I think.)

We're going to cross a river,
I explain. I'm not too experienced.
I have to meet you first, the fellow says. I haul myself to the horse

farm. He tells me right off,
Bring that big black mare into the hall.
Don't let her swing her ass to you. She'll try to pull one. Tie her like this.

He shows me. No, like this.
He shows me again. He shows me
again. Do you know left from right? I get it right.

Curry and brush her all over. All over.
Even there. Clean her feet, all four feet, he says.
Make her give you that back foot. Stay close on her rump

when you walk behind, he tells me.
If she kicks, it won't hurt so bad that way.
You get out a ways, those legs have more power, you see. Up close

it just hurts like hell. I ought
to know, he says. Keep your hand
on her haunches. Let her know where you are. Locate yourself. See this

scar? See, there's the whole horseshoe
on the side of my head. Who is this fellow,
anyhow? You met him on a computer? Was sitting on it? You sure about this fellow?

This wilderness? Now saddle her up.
You'll be all right. That's what you call tack.
Cinch that saddle, wait till she breathes out. Cinch it again. She's a smart old bitch.

Got to outsmart her. Now unsaddle her.
Don't let that stirrup drop on the far side. She'll jump
right on top of you. Pick up that foot again. Don't be timid. Let her know who's boss.

No need to be mean nor scared.
How do you know he ain't
some axe murderer? Well, yeah, I guess I could be an axe murderer. Lucky for you

I ain't. Who is this fellow?
Not my business, I know. Clean out
that mud with this pick. Watch that frog. This here's the frog.

When you going on that ride
into the wilderness? I see. Well, you
were scared. I could hear it. I could see it. It didn't

stop you though. That's what I had to know
first. If it'd stop you. I get a lot of women
your age come out here chasing some girl's lost dream about being

Dale Evans. But they're too afraid
to live, much less listen, much less tack up
a horse, grab her hoof and clean out her foot. Twice a week till time to go.

It ain't too late. It ain't about
time. It's all about your seat, how you sit
a horse. Ain't about calluses nor hours in the saddle. Not some

fancy training bullshit neither.
It's how you sit your saddle, I tell you.
You'll see. Three months go by. Before we leave, he tells the man who's asked me

to ride in the wilderness,
I don't think she'll embarrass me, but if you
forget the sandwiches, God's sakes, don't send her back alone to get nothing.

Ode to the Dixie Pig

—BUSINESS 220

God invented the barbecue
sandwich. It's a sin to eat it

without a dollop of coleslaw,
an anointment of Texas Pete.

Only vinegar-based passes
the pearly gates. God loves

takeout. This is His blessing:
a hog buried in a shallow grave

of smoldering ground, body cradled
by wet leaves covered in old tin

eating his last apple. Swab him in
vinegar and chilies,

a little brown sugar. Sop it on.
A towel made into a mop to bathe

his tangy flesh until it falls away.
Buns split and the rock slide

of potato salad tumbles onto Chinet.
God don't like doing dishes.

Note

We ride
in the Big South
Fork. I pretend it's long
ago.

Before
cars and buses.
The woods are alive. History
is real.

TV's
not invented.
Rawhide not even a
dream. The smell of horse and leather
routine.

Music
moves in the rock
of their hips and shoulders.
Hooves on dewy ground. Ears and eyes.
Time sings.

Lining Out

In the outlands, I sometimes see these young girls'
clothes hanging haphazard as their lives,
artless. No apprenticeship, only hard recourse
to troubled choices, their backless bloomers flipping

in the spring breeze for everyone to see.
That's not how it's done. Big things hang
on the ends and on the outside: sheets and towels
and bedspreads where the line's highest.

Like my grandmother's line, mine could stand
some maintenance. A lost art, hanging clothes.
Too domestic for poetry, some man poet
once told me. Bleached whites go together.

Bright colors hang like trumpet flowers
against a sheet canvas. Don't hang shirts
by the shoulders. Pray for sun on Mondays.
Iron Tuesdays. The time my slow flawless hand

caught in the wringer, Granny's hand darted cross
the air like a snake. She slammed the release. Scared me
to death. We carried wash up from the basement
in bright scarred metal dishpans to four slick bleached

white ropes waiting there like a skeleton
holding out for muscle. We hung and slapped straight
and pinched our sweet work in the shape of
our lives and waited for the sun to dry.

Deed

Becoming familiar with a body, we till, weed, mow,
doze, spray, spade, and parcel. In the warm glow

of a fading trash fire we salvage, saw, hammer, nail, brace,
side, seal. Never owned dirt before except potting soil. No past place

to plant seeds other than my womb. But your children grown,
my children grown—and glad to have us occupied, this ground

is ours to shape and swaddle. In this late-life honeymoon house, too
late to wake in the night to crying babies, still I turn toward you

like a young wife, and you reach for me, like a young husband in the
soft dark, as if we have done this all our lives here in our own geography.

Honeymoon near Oneida

Laurel blooms thick and pink in Big South Fork.
Horses' hooves tramp dewy government ground.
I imagine the old days and a little history tiptoes in.

Late spring, long before the Model T, family wagons,
buckboards, horse- or oxen-drawn, cut swaths of road
beneath the tall universe of greens, Big South Fork.

Before the bride came to Yellow Sky or the incident
at Oxbow, here were horses and hemlock. Long guns.
Buckskin and arrowhead; a little history slips in.

Lions and bears in heavenly bodies—broad hips, muscled
shoulders, heavy heads—amble earth's pitch, its sharps and flats.
Laurel's pink snow sings a chorus of the song—south fork.

Cumberland. Native son. Ears twitch and turn. Nostrils sniff, blow.
Indian Dome. Long saddle days, Tennessee to Kentuck.
I picture a time when horses were small. Time floods in.

Rain. Mud. Bear beds. Sunshine. Shade. Boar. Snake. Buck and
doe. Eyes map a wide-angle Milky Way: forest floor, river bed.
Back again. No states. These mountains echo
pink-buried dreams on the banks of an unnamed stream.

Little Farm

Our first land we broke
and shared every day like bread.
Baby goats leapt. Spun.

Hiding

Don't make me come looking for you.
Don't make me have to comb the house,
the car, the truck, the tractor, the back
of the toilet, the garage, the shed, the pile
of papers on the kitchen counter.
Where else could you be? The crappy
space beneath the couch cushions,
where you've probably latched onto
something old and sticky, down inside
the workings of the recliner where
God knows some mouse is nesting,
thinking of having babies. I know
you're watching me like so many owls' eyes,
laughing from your comfortable perches
while I search high and low, inside and out.
Sure, chuckle as I move this and that,
swipe my fingers across the dust
I can't really see anymore without you.
Amuse yourselves while I stretch
my arms out as far as they'll go
trying to read the blessed phonebook.
How can you be so cruel? To wait
patiently in your hidey holes watching
panic climb out my collar and frustration
cloud my memory all the more. I've paid
plenty for each of you, but not so much
you can afford to be coy, mean,
mischievous. You aren't prescription,
you know. You're not official.
Your elitist attitude is only as good
as what I put in front of you
under a good light. So come out, come out,
wherever you are! For pity's sake,

make yourselves useful! Or I'll drive—
something I can still do without you
sonsabitches—to Dollar General
and lay down another
Abraham Lincoln
because you need to learn
anything, I mean anything,
can be replaced.

Trail

Bubba is often mistaken
for a draft horse,
his fanny as broad
as the washerwoman's
at the end of Yellow Jacket
Cove. I trail his chestnut
rump up one sharp steep
after another. He sways
and springs forward and up
slow, as if he totes
a heavy load of wet sheets
and towels. Watch him walk
with steady step. See him push
his sleek barreled
body on fragile toothpick
legs. His steel shoes
slapping dirt and rock
toward top
steady as a ringer washer
slapping time against water,
its own momentum
getting the job done.

Two in the Morning

You open the window to the cool night.
A chill rides my arm like a train
pushing cross country, the Red Eye.

There is no moon, no stars, no hint
of a window in the pitch black. Rain
is on its way. I smell it coming as I lie

here awake, listening for the long bright
howl of the coyote who haunts lane
and vale in this hill country. He spies

the weakness in any situation. Light
or dark, early or late, he's the same,
looking for the prey that will cool

his hungry belly. His step is light,
his eyes shiv-sharp. A lame deer,
a slow calf, a weak foal, a loose pup.

I fall asleep between fear and the tight
whine of a distant car piercing my dream
of you, some wild dog, a blinding light.

Body

              Contentment
doesn't come
      with flush

toilets or electric lights

           or being able
     to get away

with fifteen miles over the limit.

            That's only glee,
and glee is temporary.

            Contentment

lasts beyond the body
          and what it needs.

Apart

There
are days
I count dishes
and glasses. The saucers
without cups. Pairs of your dime-store
spectacles surprise me as I
drift through the house—each one
evidence of
habits
you left
behind. I see
your obsessions. Ashtrays.
The faucet at the back door that
refuses to drip dry. I count
trousers in the closet.
For hours
I finger
the seat cushion,
pillow, remote, doorknob.
For minutes on end I pretend
that I float above the
carpet, some strange
reverse
magic
principle at
work, helping, keeping me
above the floor, keeping me from
counting my footsteps in any
of these lonely hollow
rooms forsaken
without
you.

Blood

red trillium and wild columbine—drips
like tiny lanterns or bells bright against
the broken leaves and twigs against
the wood rot they drip electric sometimes
the change is just a flower dripping bloody
blooms or its leaves leaving crimson
spots and scarlet stars singing with a
solar radio their red voices like carolers
beside the logging trail or dressing
the fragrant forest with costume gems
from some grandmother's jewelry drawer
scattered like sparkling crumbs something
to ask you about as we ride our tall geldings
past such slight bright bloody wounds

Fear

turns blue to orange
sours the last drops
of milk in my breast
leaves a shell of bone
my thin speckled skin
no more than a silky
mother of pearl gown
swept in static drape
making lightning
in my barren belly
this thread of deer path
the only hope this horse
and I can cling to
I grip the ground tight
with his hooves and lift
my head to clouds
before long we are dry
as old bread and implode
into fine table salt
blown away till there is
nothing left to look back

Terrain

Metal shoes slide across a round
                                   rock on the steep downhill mud.

Red does what he must
                to catch hold and fear comes

                               from my toes to my eyes,
gathering what it can

till my throat's full and I know
                              you see
                                        terror in my face.
                                                   You can't
just go on flats and ups.

I know this.   I know this.

But a steep mud-rock slope

                               changes knowledge to nothing

                    but a deep breath
caught in the snatch   of my back.

                        And what's left?

You can't let it prey

                         on you.
                             You can't think about

what might happen   till it does.

                         You've got a sure-footed horse.
                         Worry's
what kills.

Napping

in my tented sleep
your spirit comes back
to make love

you're out of your body
while it rides
the low railroad bed

plunges into
the river and mud
holes waist deep

but in the tent
you hover over me
draw me out of myself

take me back
to the dark woods
to bear dens

to ferny snake beds
the adventure of something
old and hidden and wild

feel the horse beneath us
his thoughts tremor through
his sharp shoulders

barrel belly
flanks feel the clay
road come up

through his horn-like feet
his delicate legs
ghost-travel sparkles

through his chestnut
coat he glistens and
shimmers on our behalf

December

Frozen mud crunches like glass shards
beneath my boots. Cold's sharp kisses cut

at my chapped sleep-drunk face.
Five dark muscled shadows lumber

along the fence row at cockcrow.
A thin red strip of sky rides their backs.

Pinpricks of stars cleave to the last of night.
They hear the coffee can scrape and shovel

corn and molasses. Hear the sweet feed
hail down into troughs. Thousands of pounds

gather, gear up, threaten. Ears pin flat,
thick chests heave and shove, heads sling

in this pale-lit choreography. Shod hooves
stamp frosted damp ground. Broad asses

swing. Silver-dollar-size eyes search bright
and liquid in the last drop of dark. Meanness

dances across the thick black grass
until safe in single stalls, alone, hungry,

thick lips finger what hunger counts on.
I rush back to the square of buttery

lamplight fading into dawn
to scribble the line that came

to mind in the crisp dark walk to the feedlot.
It rides my spine to my cold toes and back again,

my brittle fingers already pushing off
gloves, coat, hat to reach for the ratty

sweater, the chipped cup, afghan, notebook,
yellow pencil with its teeth-pocked scars.

Fire

Just about eight o'clock in the gray light of a damp December morning,
I sat curled like a cat on the sofa near the dots of carnival-colored lights,
a few pages into *Pharaoh, Pharaoh,* priming my pump for work.

When Christmas lights blew themselves out, I glanced up from lovely lines
and stanzas, unable to give purchase to a germinating question. The furnace
went silent as a carol without words or notes. I shoved good poetry aside

in simple search of a thrown breaker, the small mischief—electricity playing
tricks in an old cobbled-together house constructed by jackleg carpenters
making do, closing in porch after porch, adding closet after closet,

running pipe after pipe, stringing wire after wire. One step over
the threshold into the kitchen—the word I needed came ready-built
out of poplar and pine. It perfumed the holiday blaze, the smell

of a Yule log in the neighborhood where stockings might hang.
But our fireplace was past fire. Too old. Too cracked to hold heat
and cinders. I turned and ran to the shed. Breathless, I still managed

to say it matter-of-fact for my own ears. "I smell wood burning."
He dropped tools. We turned back to see the black sketch of smoke,
the thick jagged line churning from the attic of the cabin, the thick

crayoned line, something drawn by an angry child, disappointed
by Christmas morning. It was the oldest part, the best part.
Pioneers to such loss, we ran for the guns and photographs. My clothes

burned, all but what I wore. An hour later, the fire chief walked out
of the oven of our house to say, "Bruce Sevier called. Your hay's ready."
The three of us laughed, and the two of us shivered. We reached

to warm each other. We grieved for the firemen who missed Christmas
pancakes and egg casseroles, all over an old cloth-bound wire
wind-rubbed against a rusty nail, both long forgotten. Days later,

my grown son stared in subtle tears at the charred carcass of our bed
and the keyhole of a window, too small for the key of my ample hips.
Weeks later, haunted by a streetlamp, my grown daughter held me tight

on a corner a state away in a pool of winged shadows. Baptized by fire,
we were blessed and blessed. Our voices reborn, words glowed brighter
and brighter, carnival-colored embers throbbing on our unquenchable tongues.

The Letter V

V is for the child Valentine.
Her smile is a generous dialect,
vernacular of the heart chakra.

Her vocabulary comes from
the warm oven of her trust.
Her face is the shape of a heart,

even in Aries' fiery house.
Her limbs are the letters of
Be mine and *Sweetheart*.

Forest of Wordless Words

this marriage is a tree-muscled place
its network of roots going back
to the sapling of first sight
filled with sweet sway in the breeze

of laughing as we grow old
deaf and blind our history
turning to brain kisses rising
like new saplings in a new

continent tear-dazzled in private
joy a crowned lovebird chatters
as it sits in our wood-silent branches
feathering a nest of new and old

promises its blinking breastbone
a confirmation of a breathing heaven
waterfall fever of the world's eyepiece
strapped in its sun-bright shield

Spoons

Two tarnished spoons,
we lie in the dark
drawer mirroring one
another—cupped
in perfect silver-plated
fit, the curves
of our backs, the flats
of our feet, breath
to neck. How much
sugar we've shared.
The intimate sound
of sip. We fit
snug and slick,
loving and waiting
on morning
on creamer
on the strong rich
work of coffee
and first light.

Portent

A poem is a wandering dog at the door.
A stray lab mix. Timid and starving. Guarded.
Afraid and yearning, she has come
complete with her own
tension

evidenced in the dull coat, the hollow
eyes, the raised paw. Her ribs reach
for her nipples, both pointing long and empty
toward the porch—

that liminal room. A nursing mother, she looks
to you to give her water and leftovers and maybe
a towel to nest on. She doesn't require anything
expensive

or fancy. Maybe her pups will trail her scent
to the threshold where she waits. They will mew
and whine like kittens. Poems disguise themselves
if they're young and hungry.

A starving mother will set aside ego and risk all when
so much hangs on her longing. When so much rides on love
and your open door. If only she would bite, you could
be a novelist.

Mean Time

I am a ripe plum about to drop,
a watch that loses time,

a basket too full of grapes,
too full of pinecones, too full

of books, of yarn,
too full of magazines, too full

of potatoes and onions, too full
of words, too full, too full.

Some nights I am a hot plate.
The soup is boiling over.

I am a constellation of contradiction,
each star a reaction or a memory

or an epiphany that won't quit.
I am a spinning tire, spitting gravel,

a churning cloud of dust catching
the nick of time, going through

a gate, a fence, down

an endless blue line
on a disappearing map.

After the Hurricane

see it
like the body
on the cross its wings stretch
and it cries out across the bright day
see the
inky
shadow sliding
gliding across the pocked
sand its pointy fowl head slips hushed
over
the fat
rolling water
its feathered arms open
in longing it hunts for food an
empty
boot is
trapped in the wet
grit the body missing
the heel founders on its soggy
side it
says no
work today no
ladder to climb no plank
to walk no well to dig or cap
no rig
no tank
no line only
the soft speckling of sand
the tick of each pale glassy grit
against
the dead
leather etched and
scrolled with the thread wings of
birds seaweed lies

tangled and green
glistening
resting
from its rough night
the shadow slides over
again cruising for what what is
left what
can the
gull see out in
the blue ice of ocean
what can it see from its draft of
air as
it works
and works for its
living tick tick tick sand
pecks at the leather at the sole
at the
heel at
the weed at the
shadow first here then here
then there's
nothing

Altar

I ran across my *First Holy Communion Missal*
in a cedar box with a clip of my father's
obituary, his Immaculate Heart, pocketknife.

Before the cedar box, a mouse gnawed
the top of the missal's binding, white
leatherette chewed away. Creamy

signatures, thread-bound and exposed,
held prayers and pictures of the articles
of the Mass, bound together

like the wrists of a man before execution.
I reread the words: chalice, vestments,
stole, Sacred Host. Let the word *liturgy* roll

over my tongue until its light felt familiar
again. I sang *Kyrie eleison* several times.
Wished on a star in the constellation

of my family history I had protected the book
better so I could offer it to my granddaughter
on the occasion of her first Holy Communion.

But the missal and its holy contents
are too tattered to pass from my hands
to anyone's innocent tongue.

Harmonic Mean

It's the mean time. You are still too young
to worry your own death
even though she may stalk you.

You can still ride or swim or walk yourself
toward your youth
if you're dedicated.

But be mindful, gravity is subversive. No matter
how hard you work,
your chest slips slowly

toward your navel, your toes. A while longer,
dedication can mask its descent.
It is the mean time. Your life

comes crystal clear, and for once you know
your next steps toward or away
from what you have loved.

Time still feels like a tool in your hands to shape
the world. You don't admit
time is shaping you.

You still guide, still save, still sparkle.
Yet in this mean time, each day
inches closer to the tranquil abyss.

In this mean time, you decide where your life
will ripen to syrup, where
your hair will bleach out

one strand at a time. Time becomes random
vital syllables, divulging a new
harmony of words, where some open

thoughts remain beyond language. You begin
to make a friend of quiet.
Ambition pouts, impotent

on the far side of the door. At this middle place
the achievement that matters
is inside your own body.

You came to know each bird and bug as you come
now to know your own thoughts
and the thoughts that lie

beneath those thoughts and so on, where the body
becomes a reformed church
and you its solitary prayer.

Church

Let the bashful liturgy of loving
baffle you until you are unhinged

by want, frantic to clasp your ribs
round the elongated object

of your ardor. Leap up
and scramble to be first

to the water's edge. Be baptized
by the flush of His birds of kisses

rushed from their vault of reeds.
Let grace flutter and confound

your hungry heart and aching knees.
Let all your future ticks and licks

be tiny miracles that unlock mystery.
Let them be tied to the post of prayerful

rage. Rage over want. Rage over yearning.
Rage to taste and touch until bonds

snap. Let love's offertory hinge
always on some heroic happenstance.

Bedtime

At eight o'clock, Emerson
    chooses the story and slips
        between her polka-dotted

sheets. I am grateful
    for this moment alone
        with her before she dreams.

Our heads touch
    on her cloud-soft pillows.
        She smells of baby lotion

damp hair from a bubble bath.
    "I spy with my little eye,"
        she says. She is ready for words

to flutter around her
    like wings, those inky
        squiggles that architect

the pages beneath the pictures
    she loves to point to,
        Tonight it's the little rabbit

who loves to pretend
    his cardboard box
        is a rocket ship

blasting into space.
    "I have a nagination, Geekie,"
        she says and points her finger

like a wand. I read again
    and again about the little bunny's
        joy. "Be a poet," I whisper.

Mystery Rules

It begins with a singularity. Light has speed.
      Everything is star dust. Light is both wave
           and particle. Fire has its own weather. The earth

has a creamy center like a Rolo, but hot. War is heartless.
      There is no holy war. Listen for your questions. Watch
           for signs and wonders. The time for miracles

is not over. The universe is forever
      expanding. A star is a ticking bomb. Fire is good
           and bad. A black hole isn't black. Water

is self-leveling. The cosmic and the atomic look alike
      at eye level. Everything can be broken
           down to mathematics, down to dust we shall return.

You cannot eat π, but you can chew on it. Things change.
      Everything dies. Energy cannot be destroyed. The universe
           and the body strum a heartbeat. Water is wine. Wine

is blood. No man is an island. Man cannot live
      by bread alone. Bread becomes the body. Word
           becomes flesh. You are what you eat. We all eat

our words. Ask and you shall receive. The ocean speaks
      in the conch. Light depends on the observer. The Milky Way
           is both chocolate and alpha and omega particles. Without gravity

nothing sticks to nothing. Without space, all the atoms
      of the body would be a square the size of a sugar cube.
           All neutrons, all atoms, all spinning tops, all waves

in the ocean, all the world on its axis, all hearts
      on their sleeves, all galaxies speeding down the cosmic
           highway, all the universe is in motion—until the lights go out.

Galaxie Wagon

Out of the winding
ribbon of unfiltered Chesterfields

burning and floating
in switchbacks through the pitch black

lies that everything will be
all right, Perry Como croons *Dream on*

little dreamer. Dream on,
on, and on. The red-orange needle stitches

the thin light-box seam of AM
across the center dash

and the road unspools,
another ribbon or a song or a dream before

my father's sure hands,
the big steering wheel rocks a song

or a dream or
a haunting of Chesterfields glowing

their starry tips
one after another and Perry Como's

honeyed voice
slips out like a ghost through

the wing windows
with all we believed we might reach.